Winning with Growth Stock Funds

A Step by Step Guide to Investing in Growth Stock Mutual Funds with 15 Highly Effective Strategies

[:Copyright:] © 2019 by Boris Timm - amazon.com/author/boris-timm

All rights reserved. No part of this publication may be reproduced, distributed, or transmitted in any form or by any means, including photocopying, recording, or other electronic or mechanical methods, without the prior written permission of the publisher, except in the case of brief quotations embodied in critical reviews and certain other noncommercial uses permitted by copyright law.

Although every precaution has been taken to verify the accuracy of the information contained herein, the author and publisher assume no responsibility for any errors or omissions. No liability is assumed for damages that may result from the use of information contained within.

Table of Contents

Introduction 1

Chapter 1
Basic Facts About Growth / Equity Mutual Fund
Types 4

Chapter 2
Benefits of Growth Stock Mutual Funds 8

Chapter 3
Understanding Investment in the Growth Mutual
Fund 12
    This is What You Need to Do with Long Term
    Growth Stocks 14

Chapter 4
Where Would You Find Your Growth Stock? 16
    Safe Growth Stock Investments for an
    Unpredictable Market 18

Chapter 5
Growth Investing With the CANSLIM Method 24

Chapter 6
Growth Stocks Investing - A Complete Strategy
Review 31

Chapter 7
The Ultimate Investment Portfolio Hedging
Strategy 42

Chapter 8
- Strategies for Effective Growth Stock Investing ... 47
  1. Understand the Company's Business 48
  2. Know When the Company Reports Quarterly Earnings Will be Published 48
  3. Monitor the Company's Sales Growth 49
  4. Fundamentals 50
  5. Industry 50
  6. Technical Stock Charts 51
  7. Strategic Asset Class Allocation 53
  8. Balanced Sector Allocation 54
  9. Buy and Sell Strategies 58
  10. Market Timing (emotion-based) 63
  11. Research Regularly on Updates and Any Information That May Affect Your Investments 66
  12. Create an Account with a Reputable Stock Company Over the Web 67
  13. Stock Pick - Strategy on Stock Investing ... 67
  14. The Return of Diversification 69
  15. Go for Growth 71
  15+1: Get Active! 72

Chapter 9
- Investment Strategy: The Investor's Creed Revisited 74

Conclusion 82

Introduction

Have you ever considered what stock funds are? When you purchase a mutual fund, you will find that they collect a large amount of money (your money with other people's money) and invest in different types investments.

One of the investments types is the stock fund. In other words, stock funds are also known as equity funds. In this case, equity means stocks. They are similar in meaning and can be used interchangeably.

Small, Medium or Large Stocks

Stock mutual funds or stock funds have different categories. This depends on the type of stocks they (professional fund managers from the mutual fund company) mainly invest in. The types of stocks are defined by how large a company is. Whether it is small, medium or large, it makes a certain stock type.

What is Capitalization?

Then you have to know what capitalization is. Capitalization means the sum of market value of a company's outstanding stock. Usually, you will find that the total market capitalization for a small stock is less than $1 billion dollars.

Growth or Value Stocks

There is more. Stocks are then further categorized as growth or value stocks.

Growth stocks are companies that are rapidly expanding their revenues and profits. Usually, they have high stock prices relative to their current earnings or asset values.

You will find that these companies will most likely reinvest most of their profits into their company for further expansion. Therefore, it is common to see growth stocks not paying dividends.

What about value stocks? These are the stocks that are unique and in contrast to growth stocks. Usually, a good investor will look into them. They (investors) want to look for stocks that are priced lowly in relation to the profits per share and book value. You will find that the nature of value stocks is less volatile compared to growth stocks.

Some mutual funds will focus on value stocks, while others will favor growth stocks. The focus of this book is on growth stock funds. Here I will take you through a journey of a "Step by Step Guide to Investing in Growth Stock Mutual Funds with 15 Highly Effective Strategies".

Sit back, tighten your seat belt and let me give you something to expand your scope of knowledge about growth stock funds and of course grow your wealth.

Chapter 1

Basic Facts About Growth / Equity Mutual Fund Types

A growth mutual fund is a special type of fund that aims at achieving capital appreciation by investing in growth stocks. Such funds focus on fast growing companies. They are also termed as equity funds.

The mutual fund market is gaining a lot of popularity since more and more investors are looking at investing in such funds and getting better returns. A growth mutual fund is a special type of fund that aims at achieving capital appreciation by investing in growth stocks.

Such funds focus on companies that are making significant earnings or revenue growth. In simple words, you can say that they focus on fast growing companies. They are also termed as equity funds.

Types of Growth / Equity Funds

Generally growth / equity funds are divided into two categories.

Aggressive fund: This is a growth mutual fund that focuses at achieving the highest capital gains. The companies that hold such investments have a high growth potential and people investing in such funds should be prepared to face a high risk return trade off.

Conservative fund: This is exactly the opposite of aggressive funds. This fund generally targets those people who are willing to earn on a regular basis and is considered a safe, secured and non risky investment.

Selecting Growth / Equity Funds

A growth or equity mutual fund needs to be invested into after taking into consideration a variety of factors. These factors include:

Comparison of funds

Many of the funds belong to different categories like large cap, mid cap or small cap. The small caps fund target on smaller companies and have greater growth potential, whereas large cap funds have better stability. If you are a beginner, you might want to consider picking a large cap growth fund.

Choosing the fund family

Fund families are companies that assist mutual fund units to investors. It is very essential to decide the exact sponsor or fund family since factors such as fees, expenditure percentages are closely related to the fund family.

Minimum initial investment

Once you have finalized on the fund family, you might want to look at the minimum investment needed in the investing of the fund. For beginners, investing in a certain amount periodically without putting a lump sum of money would be a beneficial option.

Track record

Checking the track record both in the bear and bull market for the equity mutual funds will let you know the performance of the fund. There are many online websites that allow you to perform such analysis.

Expense ratio

Expense ratios are the expenses incurred by fund companies for managing the funds. The smaller the expense ratio, the better it will be for the investor. The expenses incurred by these companies will get directly charged to the fund.

Benefits of investing in growth / equity funds

When investing in growth mutual funds, investors get a certain amount of diversity. Since these funds only contain growth stocks, they tend to increase in specific types of economies.

Chapter 2

Benefits of Growth Stock Mutual Funds

When you are looking to invest in a mutual fund that focuses on growth, you are looking for growth stock mutual funds. This type of investment is focused on growth of the assets as opposed to an income fund where the focus is on providing a source of income through stock dividends.

The profits are re-invested into the to grow the assets of the fund, so do not expect income from this type of investment.

The investment manager will look for stocks in companies that have a large potential for growth. During hard economic times, some stocks may be bargain priced temporarily due to the state of the economy.

Such investing is highly speculative and carries with it a larger degree of risk. Make sure that you are comfortable with this risk before you invest. Fund managers also look for companies that are involved in technologies that are immature and poised for explosive growth.

Again, this is highly speculative and carries a lot of risk, but the upside is the potential for very large returns. You should also keep in mind that your money may be tied up for a considerable length of time due to the fact that many of these funds are geared towards long term growth as opposed to fast profit taking.

Funds can also be grouped according to the size of company that they specialize in. The three types are small cap funds specializing in small companies, mid cap funds specializing in mid-sized companies and large cap funds that only look at very large corporations.

The idea here is that smaller companies are capable of large growth simply due to the size and nature of a smaller business. Smaller businesses can react faster to changes in technology or marketplace. Since smaller companies also have fewer resources, they are considered higher risk because they can more easily go under in bad economic times.

The opposite holds true for larger businesses with regards to risk assessment. Larger businesses are considered to be safer investments because they have assets that can help them survive bad economic times or just bad management decisions.

As such, they typically carry a lower risk, but the downside is that they also have a lower growth potential than a smaller company.

Some funds use a mix of different business sizes, small, medium, and large corporations in order to balance the potential for growth with the amount of risk involved. Another risk mitigating strategy is investing in a larger number of companies to spread the risk more widely. The downside is more research and management fees which may impact the fund's profit ratio.

As with all types of investments, you need to assess your own financial goals. If you are an investor that can tolerate a lot of risk, then you will look to invest in a more aggressive growth fund. If you don't have money to speculate with, then you will look for a fund with more modest growth objectives, a more conservative fund that will look to minimize the potential for losses.

What Makes Value Stock Funds Different?

A value stock fund is one that invests in other securities, though in many cases it specializes in stocks. They are no different from money funds or bond funds, but they have some distinguishing characteristics, which are in this case, value and growth. They attract a high dividend rate and their objective is mainly long term performance.

Value stock funds are more common with well established enterprises, companies or corporations. Some of them actually invest in securities from different countries. Remember that the aim of these securities is to add value to your investment and as such, they seek to capitalize on diversification.

These securities may be differentiated from other types of funds like the index fund generally by the amount of management fees that is charged on them, as well as the potential for returns that they carry.

These securities are also not much different from growth funds, which invest in stocks of companies that are rapidly growing. Contrary to growth funds, value stocks do not necessarily reinvest their profits into the fund for the purpose of growth, and are very keen on paying dividends to investors. This is done on a yearly basis.

Compared to sector funds, value stocks are not discriminatory in terms of the area in which they invest. This is to say, while they look out for big and well established companies, they are non-specific on the type of industry that the company is registered under.

Sector funds on the other hand are industry specific, meaning that they either go for technology securities and utility stocks.

Chapter 3

Understanding Investment in the Growth Mutual Fund

The equity stock shares which are usually invested in some fast growing companies are called growth mutual funds. The investments in these are highly volatile and carry high risk.

The value of stock can increase steeply in the stock markets one day and could rapidly fall the next day. These growth mutual funds are good instruments as long term investments.

We can categorize the growth mutual funds in four kinds: crossover funds, aggressive growth funds, balanced funds and capital appreciation funds. The investment in aggressive growth mutual fund is risky as compared to other growth funds as they are highly volatile.

The investment in balanced fund can be made in the form of short term bonds, bonds, preferred stocks and common stocks.

These balanced funds give a regular income apart from the long term capital gains. They carry negligible risk mutual fund investment. The capital investment funds are also a form of risky investment. You can make investment in crossover funds in both private and public sectors of the equity.

The asset allocation plays a major role in getting you good returns on your investments. After you confirm the credibility, status of the company, you can finalize the asset you would want to get invested into. Make it a point to never invest in a single asset as it is risky and you may suffer immense losses if the prices nosedive.

It is always wise to divide your available finance into different assets like bonds, stocks, or funds to lessen the risk. If there is a fall in the asset value of few funds, you can possibly earn from still other assets in your portfolio. It is therefore very important to scatter your risks and thus gain stability on your investment returns.

An in-depth research on different funds and their promoters is necessary as it helps you in gathering more information on the investment status in the market. You can also consult your financial advisor or fund manager, if you are a new to the world of growth mutual fund investing.

This is What You Need to Do with Long Term Growth Stocks

Investments come in two most common categories; long and short term. Short term investments are those that can be liquidated after a short period of time, while long term ones require a long period of time before they can mature and be sold off.

Long term investments deal more with issues to do with stock selection rather than those daily decisions that are characteristic of the short term investments.

Long term growth stocks are more favorable than their counterparts because, they attract more returns. Choosing them is not an easy task and it requires some input on the part of the investor.

A few steps may guide an investor who is looking for nothing less than the best. The first step is to use what is known as a stock screen to analyze all the stocks in the market. This should be done in two levels, one of those with five year growth rates in excess of 15% and the other with those that have a compounding interest rate of 15% per year.

The next step is to put your focus on those long term growth stocks that range between $500 million and $10 billion in size. Such investments hold the potential to attract great sales in future.

Be keener to concentrate on those that hold small cap and mid cap sizes. Once you are done with this, compile those that have fast rates of growth.

Keep in mind that you cannot be able to buy all the stocks that appeal to you. This is where you have got to set boundaries or limits as an investor by narrowing down your choices even further.

If you still cannot make a sound decision, consult a fund manager who will be able to make a more simplified analysis for you. The most important point to note is that you should only purchase the stocks only when the major trend is up.

Chapter 4

Where Would You Find Your Growth Stock?

For over a century growth stocks have been a part of the financial concept. The defining characteristics of the growth stocks have changed with time, like, the 70s were signified by the tough and bearish stocks while the 80s happened to be the bullish boom period.

Apart from the basic logical analyzing, one can always refer to the financial history to obtain the formula of successful stock investing.

Zeroing down on a company with strong fundamentals, which include rising sales and earnings and low debt. This apart, one needs to take notice of a few points. They are:

- The company should belong to a growing industry.
- As an investor, you should be completely investing in stocks both during the bullish

period when there is massive price rise in the stock market and also in the general economy.

➢ You should switch most of its funds out of the growth stocks, like the technology field and pour them into defensive stocks during the bear market.

➢ You must regularly monitor your stocks. Immediately sell off those stocks that are declining and hold on to the stocks which continue to grow.

Evaluate the management of the company

Management of the company is the fundamental criteria for its success. Before investing one need to ensure that the company management is functioning well. There is a certain way in which you can check this out. They are given below but the ultimate evidence on this aspect is the rising stock price.

1. Return on equity

A quick shot to gauge the company's competence is to check the company's return on equity (ROE). ROE is calculated by dividing the earning by equity. The resultant percentage will give you a clear idea as to whether it is utilizing its equity or net assets resourcefully and advantageously. More the percentage is higher, the better it is. The company's earnings can be obtained from its 'income statement'.

This financial statement reveals the equation - sales less expenses equal net earnings (or net income or net profit). The company's balance sheet will reveal its equity. It is the total assets minus total liabilities which is equal to the net equity.

2. Insider buying

It is also advisable to check out whether the company management too is buying the company stock. After all, it is the management who best knows whether the company is really balanced for growth. If they are found buying the company stock en masse then you can rest assure regarding the growth stock potential.

Safe Growth Stock Investments for an Unpredictable Market

The stock market investing environment is certainly scary to a lot of investors in the short term. With fears of a recession on the horizon, along with problems like the falling value of the U.S. dollar, rising commodity prices, distressed credit ratings and problems with inflation, the thought of pushing new money into the stock market is definitely not a popular idea.

After testing the January lows somewhat successfully, I feel as though the market's conditions may finally be seeing improvement. In my honest opinion, we are oversold.

While the market may continue a downtrend, an oversold market is no place for shorting and reaching into the bargain bin in the first half 2008 may be the best move you ever make.

Looking into "safe" areas of the market, our selections are few and far between. Straying away from the popular markets like tobacco and discount foods, I want to highlight some areas of the stock market where high growth remains a potential and risk remains somewhat in check.

Which sub-industries am I talking about? Agriculture and Aerospace & Defense of course!

Agriculture

Out of all of the sectors in the stock market, agriculture is an investing hotbed that hasn't really slowed down or produced negative numbers for 2008. As we watched all of the pillars fall (banks, retailers, restaurants, etc.), agriculture's turn never came!

The agricultural commodities such as wheat, corn and soybeans have showed no signs of stopping their run-up, and the 2008 outlook out of these stellar companies has been nothing but positive.

Whats more? Most of these companies come with low risk, despite high upside something rare in today's market.

If you want to play this bull, and I suggest that you do, you want to keep a keen eye on Deere (NYSE: DE), Monsanto (NYSE: MON), Potash (NYSE: POT) and Mosaic (NYSE: MOS).

Let's start with Deere. I feel that they are the safest way to play this ag boom because they are an industrials sector company by definition. I recommended this company back on February 11th, and my views really haven't changed.

You aren't going to get a great valuation as they almost always trade at a premium to the market... but as long as you can catch a dip, I don't see this train slowing down any time soon.

Moving over to Monsanto, this is a fantastic investment if you can get in at an attractive price now. They recently announced a huge agreement with Becker Underwood and Plant Health Care to provide a new hybrid seed treatment platform. The Dow recently partnered up with Monsanto, and prospects are very good for the future.

Potash and Mosaic are really sitting on cloud nine right now. Even after we have seen a big drive into these companies over the past week, I think there is some space available and people really aren't being as aggressive as they should be.

Mosaic is another stock that I recommended, this one back in late January, and their catalysts haven't changed. Their PEG is over 3. Ignore it. These ag. companies don't come cheap, but I see them continuing to stride upward.

Aerospace & Defense

Being an Industrials sector buff, you can't help but feel confident in the Aerospace & Defense industry. One thing that typically will not slow in recessionary times is the growth behind military contracting, national defense funding and aerospace development.

With the ongoing war over in Iraq, there is a constant driver for most of the big five A&D firms, and much of this is guaranteed for 2008 and beyond. I like General Dynamics (NYSE: GD), United Technologies (NYSE: UTX) and Lockheed Martin (NYSE: LMT).

I want to recommend Boeing (NYSE: BA), especially with their currently dirt-cheap valuation versus their historical trading range, but I just can't see through this cloudy future.

Personally, I want to own them now, but with the disputes and such after losing a contract to a combined Northrop-Grumman and Airbus EAS team, their future is somewhat uncertain. Instead, I like General Dynamics.

Not to be cliche, but Jim Cramer recently devoted an entire segment to this A&D powerhouse. They are the biggest holding in the industrials sector of the Nittany Lion Fund, LLC that I help manage, and we are very confident in their future success.

If McCain is elected, this is a superstar. But even if he's not, this company is still secure in its fundamentals and is trading at a discount in a bullish industry.

The Aerospace & Defense industry is red hot, safe, and trading at a discount to its historical premiums despite leading the market averages this year.

With this in mind, I like United Technologies and Lockheed Martin in addition to GD. UTX recently made a proposal to acquire Diebold, which would position United Tech for some solid growth opportunities overseas. All future implications remain bullish on the stock, and analysts seem to be loving this, the biggest domestic aerospace & defense company, for the future. Lockheed Martin is your typical flawless company that continues to impress.

These folks don't disappoint and have had remarkable fundamentals and cash balance for as long as I can remember. LMT is safe and at an attractive price!

As investors, we need to look for safe havens like Agriculture and Aerospace & Defense for predictable growth, stability and recession-proofing measures in order to continue to grow our portfolios.

I wanted to touch on commodity-tied stocks like those tied to Gold, Oil and Natural Gas... but we will be touching on those soon, so we will save the best for last. Focus on the Ag. and defense companies if you, like me, can sense an oversold market with some bargain prices up for grabs.

It is one thing to catch a falling knife, but these industries really haven't fallen at all so they are ripe for investment.

Chapter 5

Growth Investing With the CANSLIM Method

The CANSLIM method was developed by investor William J. O'Neil. The method is designed so that the non-professional investor can get professional level results without having to expend the amount of time a professional does.

The method does this through growth investing as opposed to the traditional value investing. The CANSLIM method is an acronym as follows.

C = Current Quarterly Earnings
A = Annual Earnings Increase
N = New Companies, New Products, New Management, New Highs Off Properly Formed Bases
S = Supply and Demand
L = Leader or Laggard
I = Institutional Sponsorship
M = Market Direction

This method is essentially a filter which picks out growth stocks with the highest probability of increasing in value in the near future. In this method you are not looking for bargain stocks as is traditional.

You are looking for stocks with the highest chance of significantly increasing in value and that usually means buying stocks that are going up in value. Before we get into the CANSLIM method lets define growth investing.

Growth Investing Defined

Growth investors look for companies that show consistent earnings and sales growth in recent periods. Growth investors assume that a stock is accurately priced in the market and attempts to project future value based on past results and future projections.

Often growth stocks have a high price to earnings ratio because they have a record of better than average earnings growth. They typically have a high-quality product or service that brings a superior profits and return on equity.

Growth investors are not buy and hold investors. They will usually buy a stock on the way up and sell near the top, when is starts to decrease in value, or when it stops bringing a sufficient return of price increase.

Now lets talk about each of the CANSLIM criteria and how to apply them in growth investing.

C = Current Quarterly Earnings

The CANSLIM method puts a strong emphasis on earnings as that is a clear judge of a company's performance. For a company to be a growth stock they must have quarterly earnings at least 25% higher than the same quarter last year. You also want to see quarterly earnings increases in the past few quarters.

As well analyst's projections for the next quarter should be up 25%. You also want to see an increase in the rate of quarterly earnings increases. For example a 25% increase 3 quarters ago, a 35% increase to quarters ago and a 40% increase in the current quarter.

A = Annual Earnings Increase

Looking only at quarterly earnings can be misleading as companies who have had a few good quarters will be selected. To screen out companies that have not had sustained results annual earnings are factored in.

A company must have an annual earnings increase of at least 25% to be a CANSLIM growth stock. The company should have at least three years of increasing earnings to be considered. This criteria weed out companies who have short term success and will flutter out soon.

N = New Companies, New Products, New Management, New Highs off a Properly Formed Bases

A growth company should have something new that is driving its price progress. This can be a new company (less than eight years old) that has gotten the market excited, a new product that is attracting a lot of attention or new management that is operating company more efficiently or competitively.

It could also be a new high off of a base. A base is a pattern in stocks chart that shows the attention getting in the market.

S = Supply and Demand

Just like the price of anything else the price of stocks are fueled by supply and demand. A growth stock must have a high demand. There are a few ways to measure this. The best way is by looking at the stocks trading volume versus its capitalization rate.

The capitalization rate is how many shares outstanding the company has. A large capitalization stocks like Google has billions of shares outstanding. Because of this they are price progress is much slower moving because it takes a lot of buying to make a significant difference in price.

Conversely a small capitalization stock that has shares outstanding in the millions doesn't need as much volume to make big price progress. The CANSLIM method focuses on smaller capitalization stocks as they are more likely to get high demand and large price increases because of their smaller supply.

To get a good indication of a small capitalization stocks demand look at its trading volume. This is shown below the stock's price on a chart. A good sign of high demand is when a stock has more days closing up in price on higher than average volume than days is closes down in price on higher than average volume.

L = Leader or Laggard

According to O'Neil "the top one, two or three stocks in a strong industry group can have unbelievable growth, while others in the pack may hardly stir." The stocks that make the greatest price movements are leaders in their industry group.

In order to pick stocks that are going to have the greatest growth you want to know what the top industries are at the time and invest in the top companies in those groups. These are going to be the ones that will grow sooner and bigger than others.

Don't make sympathy plays as O'Neil calls them buying a second rate stock in a hot industry group hoping the "luster of the real leader" will rub off on it. The stock will eventually move up but not as much as the leader.

I = Institutional Sponsorship

The biggest buyers of stocks are large institutions such as mutual funds and pension funds. Institutions like these will regularly make trades anywhere from 1000 to 100,000 shares at a time. For a stock to be a growth stock it has to have large institutions like these buying it.

You want to look at who owns the stock and make sure at least two top institutions have significant holdings of the. As more institutions buy the stock the price will increase significantly. Google finance lists the institutions that own a stock under the ownership section.

If you subscribers to a financial paper like Investors Business Daily it will have a section which lists what institutions are buying and selling.

M = Market Direction

You can be right about all of the previous rules but if you're wrong about the direction of the general market they won't do you any good.. In a bull market three out of four stocks will go up in a bear market three out of four stocks will go down.

You want to be buying in a bull market and cashed out in a bear market. If you're doing the opposite you're swimming against the current. The best indicators of the market are major indexes.

- The Standards and poor's 500
- The NASDAQ composite
- The Dow Jones industrial average
- The NYSE composite

You want to check the indexes daily. Follow their price and volume action closely. When there is price increase on greater volume that is a bullish sign. When there is price decrease on greater volume that is a bearish sign.

That's a general idea of how to invest in growth stocks using the CANSLIM method. If you like the CANSLIM method I would highly recommend reading Investors Business Daily. It provides you with the data and research to help you be successful in the CANSLIM method without investing full time.

Chapter 6

Growth Stocks Investing - A Complete Strategy Review

Major Goals

Growth Investors are constantly trying to find tomorrow's strongest stocks. They look for companies in the early stages of their growth cycle that are already showing signs of dominance.

When they find a promising stock, they buy it even if it has already experienced rapid price appreciation in the hopes of riding the wave as the company grows and attracts more and more investors. There isn't a lot of analysis involved in growth investing, it is a criteria based strategy.

When I say criteria based, I mean Growth Investors are much more concerned with whether a company is exhibiting behavior that suggests it will be one of tomorrow's leaders than they are about the fundamental or technical aspects of a stock.

The criteria used to select growth stocks varies widely, but in general, Growth Investors are looking for companies with the potential to dominate their category and grow earnings and revenue exponentially for the next several years.

Most growth stocks offer something that gives them a unique advantage such as a cutting-edge new technology (early Microsoft... Bill almost took over the world), visionary leader (Steve Jobs at Apple... Inventions that start with an "i"), a competitive advantage (e-Bay... will they ever have competition?), or a new and unique marketing approach (Starbucks... are you selling coffee or a lifestyle?).

Investment Selection Methods

There is a little fundamental analysis and occasionally some technical analysis involved in evaluating potential growth stocks, but for the most part, Growth Investors are trying to evaluate a stock's competitive position in the market.

They won't be scared away by poor fundamentals as long as their growth stock criteria are met.

For example, if you have a startup with patents on a new technology, they are the first mover in a hot new industry, and they have a CEO with several successful startups under his belt, many Growth

Investors will buy it even if it is in debt and losing money.

One of the fundamental metrics you will hear Growth Investors talk about a lot is the Price-to-Earnings Ratio or P/E Ratio. This simple calculation is the Earnings per Share divided by the Price of the stock and the reason they love this measure is it tells you today how investors think the stock will perform tomorrow.

While some strategies would interpret a high P/E Ratio to mean a company is currently overvalued, a Growth Investor interprets this to mean that the company will earn much more in the future and that investors are simply pricing in those future earnings.

There isn't a set of rules to follow for identifying growth stocks but there are a few growth investing guiding principles that most Growth Investors adhere to. I mentioned that a growth company needs to be a leader in a new industry, so this tells you that a growth company needs to have a sustainable competitive advantage.

This can come in the form of patents, new technology, deep pockets, or first mover advantage. You also know that the P/E ratio is important and this tells you that rapidly increasing earnings is a critical piece of the strategy.

Something that goes hand-in-hand with rapid revenue growth is expense management. Revenue is great but if expenses are growing faster, profit margins begin to deteriorate, a common pitfall for many would-be growth stocks.

Finally, if a stock is going to survive the competitive early stages of a business cycle and emerge as the clear winner, it has to have great management. Growth Investors always evaluate who is at the helm.

They want to see leaders with successful track records, visionaries who are the best in their field or new and innovative business models.

This is a little off topic, but have you noticed that Growth Investing and Value Investing are basically opposing strategies? What a Value Investor would consider a great stock a Growth Investor would consider trash and vice versa.

Does this mean that one strategy is right and one is wrong? No, they have both proven to be market beaters over long periods of time for investors that get good at implementing their strategy. However, this certainly strengthens my recommendation not to mix strategies, can you imagine a Growth/Value investor? Yikes.

Risks

Growth investors will experience a lot more volatility than other strategies and the market. What does that mean? That means their stocks drop first and they drop the fastest during bearish periods.

This is due to the nature of growth stocks, many are young companies with high P/E Ratios and are viewed as overvalued during market corrections and recessions. Growth Investors have to be willing to ride out losses until the market turns bullish again.

While Growth Investing is not as technically or analytically demanding as a strategy like Value Investing, it is still a very research intensive strategy.

Growth Investors have to keep up with more than just the market, they have to know which industries, geographic regions, and stocks are hot and they also need be aware of new technologies, services and products quickly.

Successful Growth Investors are constantly shifting to different types of stocks to make sure they stay invested where there is currently a lot of interest and innovation. There is an enormous amount of information available if you're trying to figure out what's "hot" in the market right now.

Every web site, newspaper and magazine has a different opinion. Growth Investors have to be able to weed through all of this information and find the stocks that will be tomorrow's leaders.

Risk management is a tricky but critical component of Growth Investing. Many Growth Investors use buy limits and sell limits to stay disciplined and help deal with this constant balancing act.

Properly set buy limits keep them from putting money into stocks that have already experienced most of their rally and also tell them when to take a profit. Properly set sell limits will tell them when to pull their cash out of stocks that have lost as much as they are willing to risk on that particular investment.

Granted, this approach reduces your risk exposure to bad stocks, but it is disastrous if you set bad limits because growth investors lose big when their money is in cash during a rally.

Growth Stocks will significantly outperform the market during bullish periods but not if your money is sitting on the sidelines.

This is not a buy-and-hold strategy, you will trade a LOT so transaction costs can add up very quickly. A good risk management program may even require that you buy and sell the same stock several times if it fluctuates through your buy or sell limits.

Benefits

Growth stocks grow much faster than other stocks, you will significantly outperform the market during bull markets. This is the goal, Growth Investors know that if they are invested in good growth stocks during rallies, their huge gains will more than make up for the losses they experience during bear markets.

Growth Investors that get very good at risk management are more likely to sell out near the top of a stock's growth cycle, avoid buying when it's too late to get in, and sell a stock when it no longer appears to be behaving like a growth stock.

Great risk managers will have some protection against losses plus they will always have most of their money invested during market rallies.

Let's be honest, everyone wishes they had bought companies like Google, Microsoft, or Apple. Growth Investing is the strategy that gives you the best odds of hitting a home run. This is one of the few strategies that actively seeks the next powerhouse stock, the one that can grow from a startup to a Blue Chip.

This factor draws more people to Growth Investing than any other, many investors want to try to buy companies that make them feel like they won the lottery.

Long-term Outlook

Growth investing isn't going anywhere, it's a very popular strategy that always draws an enormous number of investors looking for big gains during bull markets. Great Growth Investors will outperform investors implementing just about any other strategy.

Most strategies are more conservative and provide much more protection against losses during bear markets but can't keep up with this strategy's explosive growth during bull markets because they aren't willing to take the risks involved.

One drawback of Growth Investing is that you will likely need to change strategies when you get close to retirement. As your portfolio gets much larger and as you get closer to the end of your career, capital preservation will become much more important than capital growth.

Why? For example, imagine that you're only three years from retirement and a recession hits. Since you're a growth investor, your portfolio drops more rapidly than the market and you wind up losing 40% of your portfolio.

If you're 15 years from retirement, no problem, you have plenty of recovery time, but since you're only three years away you are not likely to make up your losses and very unlikely to gain any more ground before your retirement date.

You must then decide if you would rather work longer or manage to a tighter budget during retirement. Lose-Lose decisions are no fun, smarter investors switch to a more balanced investing strategy as they near retirement.

Investor Profile

If you choose this strategy, do several hours of research per week for the first year or two so that you can more quickly develop a knack for identifying high potential growth stocks early in their growth cycle. Study history, it can tell you a lot about how great companies behaved and were viewed by the market early on. I can't stress research and work-ethic enough.

There is so much hype in the media about what stocks and industries are "hot", and successful Growth Investors are able to ignore all the hype and find stellar companies hidden amongst the rubbish. You will have to put in a lot of hard work to refine your selection criteria and develop this talent.

You will need an iron will and a strong stomach to be a Growth Investor because you are guaranteed to take losses, often very quickly, during bear markets. Successful growth investors accept this volatility as a necessary evil and ride it out while they wait for the next rally to erase their losses.

Risk management helps, but keep in mind that risk management for a Growth Investor is geared more towards timing the buying and selling of your growth stocks to maximize returns than it is toward protecting you when the market is going down.

You will usually be fully invested in high-risk stocks when a bear market hits, you'll have to accept that there will be some rough patches. These fast and sometimes large losses make it very hard for all but the strongest Growth Investors to avoid making stupid investing mistakes like panicking and selling low.

A Growth Investor's goal is to identify tomorrow's greatest companies and sometimes this can feel like trying to find a needle in a haystack, you will inevitably pick losers, especially as a beginner.

The only way to combat this is to continue refining your criteria and risk management techniques so that you pick fewer and fewer losers and get out of them more quickly as you gain experience.

You can expect spectacular gains from this strategy if you master it. Investors such as the late Al Frank crushed the market averages for over 25 years.

Granted, in some years he lost as much as 40% of his portfolio but when the market turned he made it back quickly. Investors like Al do their homework. He was one of the most disciplined and hard working investors to ever practice Growth Investing. He did exhaustive research and never stopped refining his risk management and stock selection techniques throughout his long and successful investing career.

- Value Investing: "I won't buy unless the stock is selling for less than it's worth."
- Growth Investing: "I'm willing to take some risks for portfolio growth."
- Income Investing: "This money has to last a long time, I'm playing it safe."
- Mutual Fund Investing: "I want professional expertise guiding my portfolio."
- Index Investing (Index Funds and ETFs): "I'll let the market do the work for me."
- Momentum Investing: "I want to own hot stocks until they cool off."
- Market Timing: "Ride the Bull and hide from the Bear."
- Day Trading & Technical Analysis: "I have no fear of risk, I will take big chances for big gains."

Chapter 7

The Ultimate Investment Portfolio Hedging Strategy

The first page of search engine research tells you that: "Investors use hedging strategies when they are unsure of what the market will do". Further along you learn that there are many different kinds of strategies, nearly all of which rely upon some sort of derivative betting mechanism.

But what is hedging all about in the first place?

Conspiracy theorists have their hands in the air. What's that? Portfolio hedging strategies were created to expand the market for the first generation of derivative products--- options and futures contracts.

Hedges are designed to massage your market value numbers, a kind of security blanket that softens the highs and lows of the market cycle. But why focus on the fluff of transient market values in the first place; cycles eventually correct themselves without the unnecessary drama, guesswork, risk, and trading fees.

It's not the market value of the portfolio that is of primary importance. It's the actual content of the portfolio and how you deal with the natural dynamics of the securities you own. Why can't the media reinforce that kind of stuff instead of the emotion of the month?

If a portfolio has a semi-guaranteed "base income" of 4%, a 4% cushion (or hedge) is always in place, one that grows annually with proper asset allocation management, and adds to the market value in upward cycles--- nah, too simple.

Once upon a time (long before Quants, Swaps, and million dollar bonuses) investors knew that they could not know "what the market will do"--- in direction, duration, range, or vacillation. They recognized that neither humans nor human created machines could predict the future with any degree of accuracy. So they learned how to deal with uncertainty.

They recognized the cyclical nature of the major variables that moved the market cycle, and they developed a strategy that actually worked for decades. Long-term investors navigated the peaks and troughs of the market cycle with the now obsolete, eyes wide shut, buy-and-hold approach.

This dinosaur lost its potency as soon as the markets became accessible to virtually everyone---professional investors, custodians, and trustees (in the old days) understood investing, risk vs. reward thinking, diversification, fundamental analysis, and income generation.

Cultural changes, the need for instant gratification, the pari-mutuel, product mentality of the modern investment arena, and the growth of the financial services industry brought fast and furious directional change that undermined the safety of the playing field.

Today's unprepared (but well-heeled masses) are quick to accept the candy-coated, easy to own and abuse, gambling chips distributed by the Wall Street gaming institutions and blessed by their over-lobbied senatorial henchmen.

Unfortunately, trustees, custodians, and sales professionals' job preservation instincts led them to the dark side as well.

Most people paint themselves into a market-value-only-assessment corner by investing in multi-security products and by ignoring the all-important income bucket of their portfolios.

Wall Street propaganda doesn't allow investors to focus on anything but market value, creating the need for "protective" hedging techniques.

But what do these phony insurance policies promise, and what do they actually protect?

The lack of education and general unpreparedness of newly enabled investors opens the doors for all forms of schemes, scams, techniques and hedges --- all designed to limit the bottom line impact of perfectly natural market forces.

Why do we jump through all of these "prevent-defense" hoops? Because we just don't know how or have the patience to design and manage a classic, safer, plain vanilla, stocks and bonds portfolio.

The market cycle is the favorite son of the investment gods. You either make it your friend or fail as an investor!

The ultimate investment portfolio hedging strategy is one that only requires simple to understand investment techniques like the portfolio income "hedge" described above--- part of the Working Capital Model's QDI, and the centerpiece of the Market Cycle Investment Management methodology.

The other two features of this approach (one that has guided its users through, around, and over the three financial meltdowns of the past 40 years) are explained briefly below. The "I" in QDI is for income.

"Q" is for quality. If you study the long-term behavior of Investment Grade Value Stocks, and high quality income CEFs, you'll discover that they hedge themselves more effectively than any artificial mechanism ever could.

Take a look at their histories, put a hypothetical $100 in each whenever they fall 20% from their 52-week high, and sell them when they produce a 10% profit. How many millions would you be worth today?

"D" is for diversification. Absolutely never allow any position in your portfolio to exceed 5% of total portfolio working capital (i.e., the total cost basis) and never start a position anywhere near maximum exposure.

Be honest now, how many losses would you have reduced, and how many profits would you have pocketed had you respected the QDI?

Put your investment portfolios on cruise control, with a hedging strategy approved by the investment gods.

Chapter 8

Strategies for Effective Growth Stock Investing

Regardless of your financial goals, there is a place in your portfolio for growth stocks. These are companies whose earnings are growing at an above-average rate relative to the general market.

Growth companies normally do not pay dividends, preferring instead to reinvest retained earnings back into capital projects.

While it's tempting to buy a stock based on a tip or a rumor, you'll find that it's worth doing a little more research to find stocks proving themselves with fast-growing sales and earnings.

Investment strategy is a little like religion in the financial advisor community. There are few situations that would get emotions boiling, fists flying, and require police action faster than putting a buy-and-hold advocate and a market timing zealot in a room and asking them to resolve their differences.

The truth is that most strategies work some of the time, a few work most of the time, and only Bernie Madoff figured out how to make one work all the time, right up until he got caught.

Investment strategies have two major parts: 1) what investments to buy, and 2) when to buy and sell. In this chapter I have some built-in biases, but following is an attempt to objectively look at several common strategies with a minimum of sarcasm.

1. Understand the Company's Business

It is important to understand the company's business, because doing so helps prevent you from focusing on the wrong kind of companies. Generally speaking, younger, smaller, entrepreneurial companies have the fastest growth.

Technology firms are often growth companies, because they reinvest their profits into new products and services. Older, more mature companies that are no longer innovating typically don't offer the best growth opportunities.

2. Know When the Company Reports Quarterly Earnings Will be Published

Very nearly as essential as understanding the company's business, any time you are buying a stock, it's crucial to know when its next earnings report is due. A report that misses Wall Street's views can sink a stock in no time, as investors anticipate the worst, and bail out.

On the other hand, a better-than-expected report can cause a price to spike higher as professional investors, like mutual funds and hedge funds, snap up shares. Don't underestimate the importance of earnings reports.

It helps to use a tool like Yahoo's earnings calendar when you own or are thinking of buying a stock. Almost every successful growth stock investor is in the habit of tracking earnings dates.

3. Monitor the Company's Sales Growth

As a final point, when you are thinking of buying a stock, make sure to monitor how fast its sales are growing. This can help you understand whether its earnings are driven by cost cuts, or by increasing revenue. Of course, growing revenue is the preferable reason for profit growth, as it signifies a product or service that's in heavy demand.

Don't forget this key investing step.. If you don't, you could find yourself owning stocks of companies with dwindling sales, a factor that causes professional investors to sell their shares. When that happens, the price drops.

4. Fundamentals

In the sports world they are known as statistics. They help us track performance. In the world of the stock market, fundamentals are a company's statistics. The fundamentals tell us how bad or great a company is doing. The statistics you are looking for will be labeled in categories such as: Quarterly earnings, Annual earnings, Sales growth, Profit margins, and Return on Equity. Look for the best numbers possible in each of these areas, and that the numbers are consistently improving.

That is a company you want on your team. Wait a minute that could take forever. Good News! There is a great newspaper called "Investors Business Daily" that has over 3,000 companies listed with all of their statistics. Look for companies with ratings of 90 and above, and with letter ratings of A or B.

5. Industry

Think of Industry as a player's position. If ten players are trying out for the same position, we are looking to find the very best player at their position. In the stock market similar companies are grouped together in an Industry (position) and we want to find the very best company within their industry.

We also want to find the strongest Industry to build our team around. In the NBA, for awhile the strong industry was to build your team around a big center and we had names such as: Wilt Chamberlain, Bill Russell, and Shaq.

Now we have a shift in industry to the complete athletic guard that can shoot, jump, drive, and play good defense. Names such as: Michael Jordan, Kobe Bryant, and Lebron James come to mind. In recent years we have seen Oil dominate the stock market as a leading industry, but is there a shift on the way with the need to find alternative energy resources.

Will companies involved with wind and solar energy be the next big names we hear from to drive the stock market.

6. Technical Stock Charts

Technical Charts allow us to see the historical price and volume movements of a particular companies stock. Much like we would graph the statistics of a player to track their progress and give us a visualization of their improvement, a companies stock chart will give us an accurate picture of their price performance. There are two important variables we must look at when reviewing stock charts.

First, we want to see continuous price improvement. Second, we want to see strong volume associated with the price movement as it rises. When price and strong volume are moving up in tandem it tells us that the company is very much in demand.

This strong price and volume movement is similar to that star player entering the draft and every team is scrambling to get him on their team. When we see price moving up on strong volume, it is every mutual fund, pension fund, and big bank trying to get that company on their team and they are willing to pay top price.

The best news is we can own a piece of that company, it is called stock.

Finding great growth stocks is not hard; it just requires 3 simple steps. Following the F.I.T. Plan of Fundamentals, Industry, and Technical Stock Charts will lead you to some of the very best growth stocks traded on the stock market.

These will be company's whose fundamentals shine, who are leading the way in their industry through innovation and sound business practices, and whose stock charts show technically sound patterns of reaching new price highs on strong volume.

The F.I.T. Plan helps you find the strongest and healthiest growth stocks available and may even get your investments in the best shape of their lives.

7. Strategic Asset Class Allocation

Traditional asset classes include stocks, bonds and cash. These classes are then divided into subcategories based on geographic location (U.S., developed foreign countries, emerging markets), company size (small-cap, mid-cap, large-cap), and bond style (treasuries, mortgage-backed, high-yield, etc).

Real estate, commodities, and hedge funds are sometimes added as additional asset classes. The idea behind Strategic Asset Class Allocation is to come up with a portfolio of non-correlated assets that meets an acceptable risk profile, and then stick with that allocation as the market goes up and down. The portfolio is typically rebalanced periodically to maintain the percentages of each asset class, but mostly the portfolio is left alone.

Most Common Supporting Arguments:

Easy to set up with mutual funds, which are typically aligned with asset classes.

Mutual funds provide diversification by owning many stocks with professional management.

My Rebuttal:

Many mutual fund managers tend to favor certain stock sectors at the same time, making the portfolio less diversified than it appears (e.g. overweighted in Energy or Financials).

Most stock asset classes are highly correlated when looked at over the last decade.

Semi-Objective Opinion:

Dividing the stock world by geographic location (U.S. & foreign) or by company size no longer results in a diversified portfolio. This has been a long-term trend developing and getting worse over the last 20 or so years.

As an intuitive example, when oil drops from $150/barrel to $35/barrel, all energy companies get hurt, whether they are large or small, based in the U.S. or based in Brazil. However, it is true that an asset class allocation model is easy to implement with mutual funds, and the addition of non-correlated alternative investments can improve overall diversification.

8. Balanced Sector Allocation

As stated above, a major problem with Asset Class Allocation is that the major equity classes do not behave differently enough to do an effective job of diversification. Balanced Sector Allocation gets around this by diversifying across low-correlated sectors (Technology, Energy, Financials, Healthcare, etc).

This is not a new concept. Just about any portfolio that uses individual stocks diversifies this way, and the strategy can be implemented using either individual stocks or sector-based Exchange Traded Funds (ETFs).

Most Common Supporting Arguments:

Spreading investments across non-correlated sectors does a much better job of diversification than dividing investments by company size or where their headquarters happens to be located.

Individual stocks and ETFs typically have significantly lower expenses than mutual funds.

Sector allocation can be precisely controlled.

My Rebuttal:

If Sector Allocation is implemented with a few individual stocks for each sector, there is a significant amount of company-specific risk added to the portfolio.

Semi-Objective Opinion:

In addition to showing a significant performance improvement over the last 10-20 years, Sector Allocation passes the "this just makes sense" test. Intuitively, a Healthcare stock and an Energy stock will do a better job at diversification than a large-cap Energy stock and small-cap Energy stock.

The manager of an actively-managed mutual fund is typically doing sector allocation within a particular Asset Class (e.g. Large Cap Value), but if you own several mutual funds, there is obviously no coordination between the managers.

Tactical Asset Allocation/Tactical Sector Allocation

These strategies are similar, with the difference being that one uses traditional asset classes and the other uses stock sectors. In both cases, the objective is to predict which stock class or area of the market will perform better in the near future, and overweight the portfolio to take advantage of that market segment or segments. The basis for determining which asset class or sector to invest in or stay out of can be based on a computer model, economic indicators, or (more commonly) an advisor's opinion or gut feel.

Most Common Supporting Arguments (some with questionable accuracy):

The advisor has a track record of picking the winning sectors.

When in a bear market, it's better to be in bonds, cash, or defensive sectors (e.g. healthcare).

It is possible to time the market, it's just that most people do it wrong.

My Rebuttal:

There are enough advisors trying new things that, statistically, some will be right on their predictions. When this happens, they get their own radio show. When they're wrong, you never hear about them.

Unpredictable events or government intervention can make any prediction completely worthless.

Overweighting some sectors and ignoring others adds risk.

Semi-Objective Opinion:

In order to significantly beat the market, you have to take some additional risk, and this strategy does that. When called correctly, this strategy can make huge gains. It can also lose a significant amount of money while everyone else is making money.

By picking the right sectors or asset classes at the right time, it is possible to make money in practically any environment. However, similar to flipping a coin and trying to get "heads", I'm not sure past success is a great predictor of future success.

9. Buy and Sell Strategies

A pure buy-and-hold strategy involves buying a high-quality investment such as stocks or a mutual fund, and then holding the investment through highs and lows until either your investment objectives change or you find out the investment is not as high-quality as you thought it was.

The rationale is that the overall market goes up over time, and you don't want to miss a big up day in the market by holding cash.

Most Common Supporting Arguments (some with questionable accuracy):

The majority of market gains occur on a relatively few number of days, so if you miss one of these days, your returns will be significantly less.

"Time in the market" is more important than "timing the market".

Warren Buffet is a buy-and-hold advocate.

My Rebuttal:

Missing the worst days of the market is far better than catching all of the best days. However, since no timing system exists that misses only the best days or misses only the worst days, both situations are ridiculous and using them as arguments stretches the definition of integrity.

Warren Buffet does not "buy-and-hold" like you and I would, unless you have the resources to buy a company, install the management, hold the management accountable for performance, etc.

When It Works/When It Doesn't Work:

Buy-and-hold makes money when investments go up, and loses money when they go down. Therefore, it works well during bull markets and works poorly during bear markets. For this strategy to continue to work for the next 30 years like it did the last 30 years, you have to assume that investments will continue to go up like they have during a period of economic growth that was fueled by the Baby Boom generation, an Energy bubble, a Technology bubble, and a Real Estate bubble.

Market Timing (prediction-based)

Market Timing is one of the most loosely-defined terms in the financial industry. There are many advisors who deride market timing, and yet routinely practice market timing themselves. Broadly-defined, market timing is a strategy that makes changes to a portfolio based on predicted market performance.

These changes may involve selling all investments and moving to cash, or simply adjusting the percentage of stocks and bonds because of economic conditions or anticipated market behavior. Prediction-based market timing bases decisions on an advisor's assessment of future conditions.

If high-inflation is anticipated, investments that hedge against inflation would be added. If economic contraction is anticipated, an advisor might move to a heavier cash position. Most Common Supporting Arguments:

By using indicators such as inflation, unemployment, factory usage, etc, it is possible to anticipate which sectors have a higher chance of outperforming in the future.

My Rebuttal:

Economic indicators work when nothing interferes with them, but unexpected events such as government action or national conflict override any statistical probability used for predictions.

Overweighting some sectors and ignoring others adds significant risk to a portfolio.

When It Works/When It Doesn't Work:

This method is highly dependent on the person or statistical model making the prediction. If the predictions are accurate, this strategy has a good chance of significantly outperforming other methods.

If the predictions are wrong, the opposite is true. Because of the large number of advisors who make predictions, a certain number will get it right several times in a row, but statistically this will not indicate any greater likelihood that they will continue to be right in the future.

As mentioned above, unanticipated news events or government action will instantly derail most statistical models.

Market Timing (momentum-based)

Momentum-based market timing uses technical indicators (stock charts and current market behavior) to determine whether the market is in a downtrend or an uptrend. Downtrends occur when more people want to sell than want to buy, and uptrends occur when more people want to buy than want to sell.

Price movement and trading volume can determine whether there is more buying pressure or more selling pressure at any given time, and the theory behind momentum is that once a trend is in place, it tends to stay in place. For how long? Until it stops.

Most Common Supporting Arguments:

Price movement and trading volume offer strong clues about buying pressure and selling pressure, and whether large institutional traders are buying or selling.

Institutional traders do not establish or eliminate entire positions in a single trade, and typically spread trading over several days or weeks. Therefore, trends tend to stay in place for some period of time once they are established.

My Rebuttal:

This makes a lot of sense to me, so I don't typically argue against it. However, it has some weak points (see below).

Some advisors can go over-board on technical patterns (head and shoulders, cup and handle, shallow birdbath with a floating stick...I made that one up). These advisors are traders looking for short-term movements. Trends, on the other hand, are determined more by a pattern of higher-highs or lower-lows, and it doesn't need to be very complicated.

When It Works/When It Doesn't Work:

There are some key components required for this system to work.

a) The method for determining trends must not be too early or too late. Stocks seldom move in a straight line. They typically make a strong move, and then rest or pullback.

Assuming too early that a trend is being established or ending will result in jumping in or out during pullbacks or corrections. Waiting too long or for too many confirmation signals will result in missing a good portion of the trend.

b) Investments must be liquid. You must be able to act when your system tells you to buy or sell.

c) Whether you use Moving Averages, charting, or any other system to determine a trend, the trend will not always hold. Each system will break down under certain conditions, so the objective is to use a system that works under the widest set of conditions and/or breaks down under the narrowest set.

10. Market Timing (emotion-based)

This is not a strategy that is typically planned for or entered into intentionally, and is the form of market timing most often practiced by those who swear they hate market timing.

Many practitioners of this strategy consider themselves to be buy-and-hold investors, but they end up moving to cash when the pain gets too great or the market is too scary. Typically, this happens after a significant loss is already on the books, which actually makes this a form of momentum.

The rationale is that if my investments have already lost money, they may continue to lose money. The problem is that if emotion or fear drives the sell decision, then the decision to get back in is typically based on "feeling better", which almost always happens at a higher price than the sell price.

Most Common Supporting Arguments:

Not too many people are active proponents of this strategy, but a lot of people practice it.

My Rebuttal:

Not much to rebut, other than pointing out that you can't call yourself a buy-and-hold investor if you move to cash or change your stock allocation when the market gets scary, and no one should use this method as an example to "prove" that all market timing systems are doomed to failure.

When It Works/When It Doesn't Work:

This strategy seldom works, and is the reason that the vast majority of investors buy when the market is high and sell when the market is low. It doesn't matter which strategy you use; just about anything is better than basing investment decisions on emotion.

Disclosure (my bias)

I use a Balanced Sector Allocation strategy using low-correlated ETFs, and momentum-based market timing. The objective is to participate as much as possible in uptrends, and avoid as much of the downtrends as possible. This requires a set of rules that makes the decision points unemotional.

A Balanced Sector Allocation guarantees participation in the hottest trending sector at any given time, but with a mechanism to get out of a sector when it starts heading back down.

Weak Points:

Because it takes a little while for a downtrend to show itself, sell decisions will never happen right at the top of a trend. The same holds true for uptrends and buy decisions. If the market gets indecisive and swings far enough that it keeps looking like uptrends and downtrends are forming but no follow-through happens, a condition could occur where losses are exaggerated. This would be a very specific and narrow set of conditions, and I have other checks that attempt to minimize this condition, but it still exists.

A very important technique when engaging in stock-trading is to get sufficient education not only on how to trade with stocks, but also about the different market movements, what factors can affect the market and your chosen stocks, and so on.

Playing the Stock market based only on speculation and guesses is definitely a huge no-no. All newbie traders should not skip on this vital stock investment advice of learning everything there is about stocks, the market, and, of course, must-use stock trading strategies.

11. Research Regularly on Updates and Any Information That May Affect Your Investments

When you're into stock-trading, it is also of the utmost importance to research on market trends, events that can affect your trades, and many more.

Whenever you trade with stocks, you have to see to it that you're always updated on stocks information, any changes in the market, etc, as those information can help you make the right decisions when you're playing the Stock market.

Remember this essential stock investment advice as well: prior to choosing any set of stocks, make certain that you've researched well about the company, the productivity of that company, and the likes, so that you are assured that you're investing in the right stocks.

12. Create an Account with a Reputable Stock Company Over the Web

Included in the list of stock trading strategies is for you to set up an account with a reputable or trusted stock company over the Internet. You need an online account so you can start to trade with stocks.

Before signing up with any stock-company, however, check on its feedback, reviews, and reputation, as it is important that you own an account with a stocks company that can really give you good service.

Remember that online stock companies are where you can receive tools for analysis of your trades, stock charts, and so on, thus, a stock investment advice you should not forget is to carefully choose your stock-company.

13. Stock Pick - Strategy on Stock Investing

Stock pick is the key of stock investing. With many stocks out there, we need to know which stock we should buy, and which stock we should sell. If you choose well, then you'll reach glory, if you choose the wrong stock then you might just say goodbye to your money. So how do you choose?

If you want to go somewhere like your home, there's maybe many roads you can choose. Different roads have also different characteristic.

You'll most probably choose the road which you like the characteristic. If you like the mountain scenery, you might want to go though the mountains.

The same like that example, stock picking is very crucial. It's actually the key for success, and the guide for glory. Just follow and stick with your stock pick guide, and you'll reach your goal.

But remember that there's no guarantee that your stock pick strategy will be 100% accurate, because there's a lot of factor which influence a company performance, and many of it is tangible like brand, employee competence, and human emotional.

Many people use screener as a strategy to pick stock. There are many popular screener, like Graham screener for the value investing method. You can modify the screener to fit your character.

If you are risk averse or risk taker, you can change the screener to increase the effectiveness. Other people uses software like Vector2000 Stock Systems which gives advanced technical analysis and market forecasting for short term stock market trends, c/w trade recommendations, timing indicators, enhanced quotes / charts and MarketMeter. These software is made by expert which can make life easier.

14. The Return of Diversification

We believe that effective diversification becomes more important in an environment of rising volatility. We expect the interrelationship of stocks and bonds to provide more diversification benefits than in past cycles as real interest rates become the driver of relative performance.

Correlation measures the degree to which asset returns move together or in opposite directions. Over time, the correlation between two asset classes can change. For instance, the relationship between the total returns of stocks and the total returns of bonds has varied over the past 75 years.

During much of the 1980s and 1990s, stock and bond prices generally moved together, as reflected in the +0.5 correlation between them over the period.1 In the 1990s, diversification offered little value to investors - stocks and bonds generally moved in the same direction.

In contrast, the correlation between stocks and bonds in recent years - just as in the 1950s - has reversed, reaching -0.5. Diversification is of more value in managing volatility now than at any time in the past 40-50 years!

The recent decline in the stock market was mirrored in a decline in yields (and rise in bond prices) as market participants' expectations for economic growth were tempered. Indeed, since the peak in the S&P 500 on July 19, the intermediate term government bonds have gained about 5% while stocks have fallen about 5%.[2]

We expect the correlation between stocks and bonds to remain below the levels seen in the 1980s and 1990s. In an era of a low, stable pace of inflation relative to historical levels, the volatility of interest rates may be driven more by expectations for the real rate of economic growth than by inflation expectations.

In general, rising inflation tends to be a negative for both stocks and bonds. In contrast, rising real growth is a plus for stocks but a negative for bonds, because bond yields generally rise and prices fall.

A similar period of negative correlation between stock and bond prices resulting from low and stable inflation occurred in the 1950s and 1960s.

A benefit of the changing correlation between stocks and bonds is that as price volatility remains elevated in the years ahead, a lower-than-average correlation between stocks and bonds should produce more benefits from diversification, which should serve to moderate overall portfolio volatility.

15. Go for Growth

In recent years, it was easy for investors who didn't periodically rebalance their portfolios to become over-weighted in value stocks - dominated by the financial sector, which is at the hub of the current market turmoil.

With the exception of the aftermath of the technology bubble in the early 2000s, value stocks have tended to be more cyclical than growth stocks - meaning they display greater volatility when economic growth slows.

As volatility has returned to the financial markets growth stocks have displayed less volatility than their value peers.

We expect better performance by growth stocks in the years ahead. In contrast to the 1990s, the excesses that have built up during the 2000s business cycle can be found in value rather than growth stocks.

For example, the energy sector has soared along with energy prices and is vulnerable to a pullback in prices from record highs and the financial sector is exposed to the aftermath of the bubble in subprime debt. The large cap growth asset class is more attractively priced than any time in the last 10 years and earnings growth is likely to remain robust.

15+1: Get Active!

Active managers benefit in an environment of rising volatility. The percentage of active managers beating their index tends to rise and fall with the trend in market volatility. During the second half of the 1990s economic cycle, volatility steadily rose - as did the percentage of large cap managers beating the market.

The percentage of large cap managers beating the index rose steadily along with volatility from 11% at the end of 1995 to 68% by the end of the first quarter of 2001.3 As volatility remains elevated relative to recent years, we may look forward to stronger relative performance by managers relative to their indexes.

While the return of volatility may be unwelcome by some market participants - it may actually be good news. The turnaround in volatility has historically been followed by years of additional gains before the end of the business cycle.

A focus on diversification, large cap growth stocks, and active management can help to effectively manage portfolio volatility. In addition, we believe that rising volatility presents opportunities to potentially enhance return and manage risk through tactical asset allocation shifts.

Rather than ignore volatility and adhere to a rigid allocation, we seek to capitalize on market volatility and make full use of the flexibility of our asset allocation framework.

1 S&P 500 and the Ibbotson Intermediate Term Government bond index

2 Ibbotson Intermediate Term Government bond index

3 Chicago Board Options Exchange Volatility Index; large cap core managers in Lipper database.

Chapter 9

Investment Strategy: The Investor's Creed Revisited

Fascinating, aren't they, these security markets of ours, with their unpredictability, promise, and unscripted daily drama? But individual investors themselves are even more interesting. We've become the product of a media driven culture that must have reasons, predictability, blame, scapegoats, and even that "four-letter" word, certainty.

We are becoming a culture of speculators, where hindsight is replacing the reality-based foresight that once was flowing in our now real-time veins. Still, the markets have always been dynamic places where investors can consistently make reasonable returns on their capital.

If one complies with the basic principles of the endeavor and doesn't measure progress too frequently with irrelevant measuring devices, growth in working capital, market value, and spendable income are quite likely to happen without undue risk taking.

The classic investment strategy is so simple and so trite that most investors dismiss it routinely and move on in their search for the holy investment grail(s): a stock market that only rises and a bond market capable of paying higher interest rates at stable or higher prices. This is mythology, not investing.

Investors who grasp the realities of these wonderful (speculation driven) marketplaces recognize the opportunities and relish them with an understanding that goes beyond the media hype and side show "performance enhancement" barkers. They have no problem with the "uncertainty"; they embrace it.

Simply put, in rising markets:

When investment grade equity securities approach the "reasonable" target prices you have set for them, realize your profits, because that's the "growth" purpose of investing in the stock market.

When your income purpose securities rise in market value the equivalent of one-year's-interest-in-advance, take your profits and reinvest it in similar securities; because compound interest is the safest and most powerful weapon we investors have in our arsenals.

On the flip side, and there has always been a flip side (more commonly dreaded as a "correction"), replenish your equity portfolio with now lower priced investment grade securities. Yes, even some that you may have just sold weeks or even months ago.

And, if the correction is occurring in the income purpose allocation of your portfolio, take advantage of the opportunity by adding to positions, increasing yield and reducing cost basis in one magical transaction.

Some of you may not know how to add to those somewhat illiquid bond, mortgage, loan, and preferred stock portfolios quite so easily. It's time you learned about closed end funds (CEFs), the great "liquidators" of the bond market. Many high quality CEFs have 20 year dividend histories for you to salivate over.

This is much more than a "buy low, sell high" oversimplification. It is a long-term strategy that succeeds... cycle, after cycle, after cycle. Do you wonder why Wall Street doesn't spend more time pushing its managed tax free income, taxable income, and equity CEFs?

Unlike mutual funds, CEFs are actually separate investment companies with a fixed number of shares traded on the stock exchanges. The stock can trade (real time) above or below the net asset value of the fund.

Both the fees and the net/net dividends are higher than any comparable mutual fund, but your advisor will probably tell you they are more risky due to "leverage".

The leverage is short term borrowing and is absolutely not the same as a margin loan on the portfolio. It's more like a business line of credit or a receivables financing tool. A full explanation can be found here:
https://www.cefconnect.com/closed-end-funds-what-is-leverage

I'm sure that most of you understand why your portfolio market values rise and fall throughout time... the very nature of the securities markets. The day to day volatility will vary, but is generally most noticeable surrounding changes in the longer term direction of either market, income purpose or growth purpose.

Neither your "working capital" nor your realized income need be affected by the gyrations of your market value; if they are, you are not building a "retirement ready" portfolio.

So rather than rejoicing through each new stock market rally or lamenting each inevitable correction, you should be taking actions that enhance both your working capital and its income productivity, while at the same time, pushing you forward toward long term goals and objectives.

Through the application of a few easy to assimilate processes, you can plot a course to an investment portfolio that regularly achieves higher market value highs and (much more importantly), higher market value lows while consistently growing both working capital and income... regardless of what is happening in the financial markets.

Left to its own devices, an unmanaged portfolio (think NASDAQ, DJIA, or S & P 500) is likely to have long periods of unproductive sideways motion.

You can ill afford to travel eleven years at a break even pace (the Dow, from December 1999 through November 2010, for example), and it is foolish, even irresponsible, to expect any unmanaged approach to be in sync with your personal financial objectives.

The Investor's Creed

The original "Investor's Creed" was written at a time when money market funds were paying above 4%, so holding uninvested equity bucket "smart cash" was, in effect, a compounding of profits while waiting for lower equity prices.

Income bucket cash is always reinvested ASAP. Since money market rates have become minimal, equity "smart cash" has been placed in tradeable equity CEFs with yields averaging over 6% as a replacement... not as safe, but the compounding makes up for the increased risk over money funds.

It sums up several basic asset allocation, investment strategy, and investment psychology principles into a fairly clear, personal portfolio management direction statement:

My intention is to be fully invested in accordance with my planned equity/fixed income, cost based, asset allocation.

Every security I own is for sale at a reasonable target price, while generating some form of cash flow for reinvestment.

I am pleased when my equity bucket cash position is low, signaling that my assets are working hard to meet my objectives.

I am more pleased when my equity bucket cash is growing steadily, showing that I've been capitalizing all reasonable profits.

I am confident that I'm always in position to take advantage of new equity opportunities that fit my disciplined selection criteria.

If you're managing your portfolio properly, your cash + equity CEF position (the "smart cash") should be rising during rallies, as you take profits on the securities you confidently purchased when prices were falling. And, you could be chock full of this "smart cash" well before the investment gods blow the whistle on the stock market advance.

Yes, if you are going about the investment process with an understanding of market cycles, you will be building liquidity while Wall Street is encouraging higher equity weightings, while numerous IPOs are taking advantage of euphoric speculative greed, and while morning drive radio hosts and personal friends are boasting about their ETF and Mutual Fund successes.

While they grow their hat sizes, you will be growing your income production by holding your income purpose allocation on target and salting away the growth purpose portion of your profits, dividends, and interest in an equity based alternative to "de minimis" money fund rates.

This "smart cash", comprised of realized profits, interest, and dividends, is just taking a breather on the bench after a scoring drive. As the gains compound at equity CEF rates, the disciplined coach looks for sure signs of investor greed in the market place:

Fixed income prices falling as speculators abandon their long term goals and reach for the new investment stars that are sure to propel equity prices forever higher.

Boring investment grade equities falling in price as well because it is now clear that the market will never fall sharply again... particularly NASDAQ, simply ignoring the fact that it is still less than 25% above where it was nearly twenty years ago (FANG included).

And the beat goes on, cycle after cycle, generation after generation. Will today's managers and gurus be any smarter than those of the late nineties? Will they ever learn that it is the very strength of rising markets that, eventually, proves to be their greatest weakness.

Isn't it great to be able to say: "Frankly Scarlett, I just don't care about market directional changes. My working capital and income will continue to grow regardless, possibly even better when income purpose security prices are falling."

Conclusion

When you are considering investing your money on trading in the stock market, you may want to plan out your strategies and focus on practical forex training. Having a strategy in how to trade and deal within the stock market would require you to have the right information on what stock market trading entails.

That is why it is important to gather information that can allow you to understand how trading in the stock market is done and this goes the same for those that wish to learn forex trading.

Allow me to recommend my books to you for more detailed information about investment in stocks:

1. A Simple Guide to Investing in Turnaround Stocks
2. Options Trading Basics Explained

With the above books you are almost sure of having a compendium of resources in stock market information.

Informed investors who want to put their money to work to earn higher returns invest in stocks. Unless you are an experienced stock picker who really knows how to invest, your best option is to invest in stock funds. Unless you get investor tips from a real pro or pay for advice, picking stock funds to invest in is your job.

Information is key in this game. Grab the keys here.

Once some of the information becomes financially useful to you, do me a favor by sharing the books with your family and friends so that wealth can go around.

From the author's desk: Reviews are gold to authors! If you've enjoyed this book, would you consider rating it and reviewing it on Amazon.com?

www.ingramcontent.com/pod-product-compliance
Lightning Source LLC
Chambersburg PA
CBHW031924170526
45157CB00008B/3045